International Federation of Library Associations and Institutions
Fédération Internationale des Associations de Bibliothécaires et des Bibliothèques
Internationaler Verband der bibliothekarischen Vereine und Institutionen
Международная Федерация Библиотечных Ассоциаций и Учреждений

IFLA Publications 36

Guidelines for Public Libraries

Prepared for the
IFLA Section of Public Libraries

K · G · Saur
München · New York · London · Paris 1986

IFLA Publications
edited by Willem R. H. Koops

Recommended catalog entry:
Guidelines for public libraries / prepared for the IFLA section of public libraries. –
München, New York [etc.] : K.G.Saur, 1986. – 91 p.; 21 cm. –
(IFLA Publications ; 36)
ISBN 3-598-21766-8

CIP-Kurztitelaufnahme der Deutschen Bibliothek

Guidelines for public libraries /[Internat. Fed. of
Library Assoc. and Instituitions] . Prepared for the
IFLA Sect. of Publ. Libraries. – 3. ed. – München ;
New York ; London ; Paris : Saur, 1986.
(IFLA publications ; 36)
Bis 2. Aufl. u.d.T.: Standards for public libraries
ISBN 3-598-21766-8

NE: International Federation of Library
Associations and Institutions: IFLA publications

© 1986 by International Federation of Library Associations
and Institutions, The Hague, The Netherlands
Printed and bound in the Federal Republic of Germany
for K. G. Saur Verlag KG, München
by Strauss Offsetdruck GmbH, Hirschberg
by Buchbinderei Schaumann, Darmstadt
Typesetting: SatzStudio Pfeifer, Germering

ISBN 3-598-21766-8
ISSN 0344-6891 (IFLA Publications)

CONTENTS

PREFACE

The Public Libraries Section of IFLA last published *Standards for Public Libraries* in 1973. They were reprinted with a few minor amendments in 1977. Since then many changes have occurred, world-wide, in the resources available for public library development and in the public expectation of library services. The Section therefore thought it timely to look afresh at its 'standards', and in 1983 appointed a working group for that purpose. The work of the group has inevitably been carried out mainly by correspondence, and no individual member should be assumed to agree with every point in the Guidelines which have emerged. The report of the working group was presented at the IFLA General Conference in 1985.

Membership of the Working Group

The following members were nominated by the Section of Public Libraries, or were subsequently invited to join the Group to provide a more balanced representation of interests:

Friedrich Andrae	Federal Republic of Germany
Eva Brown	United States of America
Gloria Dillsworth	Sierra Leone
Reynaldo Figueroa Servin	Mexico
István Papp	Hungary
Jes Petersen	Denmark
Ilse Schumann	German Democratie Republic

The following additional members were nominated by Sections and Round Tables of IFLA:

Section of Children's Libraries	Eva Glistrup (Denmark), Lioba Betten (FRG)
Section of Libraries for the Blind	Winnie Vitzansky (Denmark)
Section of Libraries Serving Disadvantaged Persons	Jean Clarke (United Kingdom)
Round Table: AV Media	Anna Johansen (Denmark)
Round Table: Library Service to Ethnic and Linguistic Minorities	Michael Foster (United Kingdom)
Round Table: Mobile Libraries	Peter Heise (Denmark)

Coordinator: Arthur Jones (United Kingdom)

DEFINITIONS

The following terms have been used in this volume:

PUBLIC LIBRARY. A library established and financed by a local – or in some cases, central – government body, or by some other organization authorized to act on its behalf, available without bias or discrimination to all who wish to use it.

PUBLIC LIBRARY SERVICE. A general term which refers to the functions or output of a public library, not to its organization or administrative control.

ADMINISTRATIVE UNIT. Any independent library, or a group of libraries, under a single director or a single administration.

LIBRARY AUTHORITY. The governing body responsible for providing public library service within a single administrative unit – usually a local authority or municipality.

PUBLIC LIBRARY SYSTEM. A group of public library services and service points which is managed collectively, with shared staff and administration, and a stock of books and other materials held in common. A public library system will usually constitute a single administrative unit, but two or more administrative units may find it convenient to cooperate to provide a single public library system.

SERVICE POINT. One of the points in a public library system where members of the public may obtain access to the public library service. It may be a main, regional, district or branch library, a mobile library, a deposit collection, or a special service point in a hospital, prison or other institution.

> *This definition extends, but does not conflict with, the ISO definition of service point: "Any library at which is provided in separate quarters a service for users, whether it is an independent library or a part of a larger administrative unit".*

DATABANK. An organized collection of information. The term is usually applied to a collection held in machine-readable form in a computer store.

DATABASE. A file of bibliographical records held in machine-readable form in a computer store.

> *In this volume the term "databank" is used in preference to "database" when either would be appropriate.*

OBJECTIVES, GOALS, These terms have not always been used consistently. In this volume the word OBJECTIVES is used to describe the purpose or end-product of the services provided by the public library; GOALS are successive levels of achievement in pursuing those objectives. (See page 8, and paragraphs 5.2–5.3).

INTRODUCTION

The Unesco Public Library Manifesto* identifies in broad terms the objectives of public libraries:

To contribute to lifelong universal education

To facilitate appreciation of the achievement of humanity in knowledge and culture

To be the principal means whereby the record of man's thoughts and ideas, and the expression of his creative imagination, are made freely available to all

To refresh the human spirit by the provision of books and other media for relaxation and pleasure

To assist students

To provide up-to-date technical, scientific and sociological information

Those then are the directions in which public libraries are moving. This volume offers guidance as to the routes they might follow in pursuing their objectives.

NEEDS

Public libraries exist to meet the needs of communities which differ widely in their circumstances and composition, and in the economic resources at their disposal. Some consist predominantly of elderly and retired people, others of families with a high proportion of young children. Some people are engaged mainly in agriculture in sparsely populated rural areas, others work in commerce or industry in crowded inner cities; some live in affluence, others in poverty.

All need access to books and other media for purposes of education or recreation, or to assist in their day-to-day activities. All need information, of which the public library is often the most accessible source. Even in the most affluent areas, the resources available are seldom sufficient to meet every one of these needs fully. Within each library therefore priorities must be determined, and immediate and long range goals must be selected in the light of local needs and resources.

* See Appendix I

9

INTERNATIONAL GUIDELINES

When needs and resources vary so widely there can be no common standards for services. For that reason we have called this volume not "standards" but "guidelines". We are offering not rules but advice, based on experience drawn from many countries and capable of general application. This is not a comprehensive manual of library practice, but we hope that it will be a useful tool for anyone concerned with the provision of public library services. We have tried to identify the many decisions which must be taken in establishing and managing such services, and have begun by providing a detailed checklist of services and facilities which a public library might properly consider providing.

It is the task of library authorities and their chief librarians to assess needs, determine priorities, and quantify the resources required to meet the needs of their communities. Recommendations as to desirable levels of provision, based on past experience in quite different circumstances, are bound to be unreliable and misleading. We have therefore made no recommendations regarding areas of buildings, numbers of staff, or the quantities of books and other materials which libraries of different kinds should provide. We have discussed these questions in general terms, and have summarized in an appendix the quantitative recommendations which were contained in the 1973/77 editions of *Public Library Standards*. We have also tabulated in a second appendix some figures relating to the provision and use of a selection of libraries from many countries.

This volume does not explain in any details *how* to do things: it is more concerned to suggest *what* might be done. It is supplemented by the more detailed recommendations on certain specific services, which have been published by specialized groups within IFLA's Division of Libraries Serving the General Public. These have been listed in a third appendix.

HOW TO USE THESE GUIDELINES

We recognize that these guidelines will probably be of greatest value in library systems which are in their early stages of development. However, it is likely that no system is currently engaged in all the practices to which we draw attention, and many will not even have given serious consideration to some of them. We believe therefore that everyone responsible for the provision of public library services will find some value in perusing this volume.

The working group identified many imperatives and felt strongly on many issues: the words "must" and "should" occur frequently. Nevertheless this is not a set of rules for designing an ideal library service: it is a tool to help in the development of services which will best meet the needs of your own community. The guidelines will suggest what might be possible, but local conditions will dictate what is feasible, with regard both to services and to organization. When desirable changes in provision have been determined, the guidelines offer further assistance in putting the changes into effect.

ARTHUR JONES

Chapter 1

PUBLIC LIBRARY SERVICES

This chapter reviews the services which public libraries commonly provide, or might consider providing, in pursuit of their objectives. It has been placed first because an appreciation of the potentiality of public libraries must precede any consideration of the provision and management of required resources.

Public libraries should be equally available to all members of the community, regardless of race, colour, nationality, age, sex, religion, language, status or educational attainment. Place of residence or the possession of physical handicaps should also be no bar to full access to library services: when readers cannot come to the library, it may be necessary to take the library to them. Resources, however, are never limitless. They must be carefully deployed to give maximum benefit to their communities. Each library authority therefore elects to provide a range of services whose variety and depth best suit local needs: the allocation of resources should be based on an assessment of the needs of the local population as a whole, not solely on the demands of present library users.

The communities which public libraries exist to serve include many people who are not library users, and who may never become users unless their needs are identified, anticipated and provided for. The services must be positively promoted and advertised so that people can begin to appreciate how libraries can help to meet their needs. Close links with local press, radio and television, with special interest groups of all kinds, and especially with schools, will all be helpful in this. Thus, "market research" and "marketing" are two underlying services which help to ensure close links between a library and its community. Without them other services will fail to achieve their full potential.

The original function of a public library, to provide a collection of books and periodicals for use both on the premises and elsewhere, has become the nucleus of a wide range of facilities. It varies from place to place and often supports, or merges with, services provided by other cultural, recreational, educational and social services and agencies. Factors which have stimulated the introduction of additional services by the public library include:

The increasing variety of media of communication, and of methods of presentation and reproduction.

A wish to exploit the library's collections, and satisfy the interests of users, by such means as lectures, exhibitions and publications.

The logical extension of the information function of the library to provide a comprehensive information service for the community.

Greater understanding of the needs of groups and individuals, and a more imaginative assessment of the contribution which public libraries can make to meeting them.

Recognition of the value of closer links between the library and its community.

The importance of making the maximum possible use of library buildings for a wide range of community purposes.

A CHECKLIST OF SERVICES

The following services merit consideration when public libraries are being planned or developed. Many are already provided as a matter of course, others are less familiar. Some involve expenditure, but many consist in the more purposeful use of facilities which are already available.

Lending and reference materials

1.1   Books and periodicals, sound recordings, video recordings, games, computer programmes, pictures, and other audiovisual materials, for loan to individuals or to groups.

1.2   Quick reference books and information files for use on library premises.

1.3   A collection of standard works, and audiovisual materials of various kinds, for reference and research use on library premises. The extent of this collection will depend on the size of the library.

Aids to borrowing

1.4   Catalogues to identify and locate the material available; bibliographies to identify wider resources; booklists on specific subjects for consultation, purchase or free distribution.

1.5   The opportunity for users to request and reserve books or other materials not in stock or not immediately available; a commitment by the library to obtain such materials quickly on request and to inform enquirers when they are ready for collection.

1.6 Equipment to enable users to examine the contents of audiovisual materials before borrowing them, and staff to check their condition on return.

1.7 Trained staff to assist in the identification and selection of material.

Aids to reference and study in the library

1.8 Study desks with shelves for books and supports for papers, power points for audiovisual equipment, and a degree of enclosure to reduce distraction and increase privacy.

1.9 A number of cubicles or carrels for study projects which involve the long-term use of many books and materials.

1.10 Slide projectors, tape recorders, cassette players, video recorders, microform readers, magnifying glasses, various aids for handicapped people. It may sometimes be possible to lend equipment of this kind for use in the home.

Lending and reference services for children

1.11 Provision for children will follow the same general pattern, but their needs should be separately assessed in relation to each point in the list.

Information services provided by library staff

Determine policy regarding the provision of information in the following categories:

1.12 Short factual answers, drawing mainly on "quick reference" books.

1.13 Information requiring more detailed research, including the correlation of material from different sources. Some work of this kind is commonly undertaken by library staff, but a point may be reached where further searching must be undertaken by the enquirer. Circumstances may arise in which the library could undertake protracted research for an enquirer only on a consultancy basis, involving the payment of a fee.

1.14 An "in depth" information service in specific fields, possibly related to the needs of local commerce and industry. If it is to inspire confidence, such a service will probably need staff with specialized training and experience in addition to a qualification in librarianship.

1.15 Community information, provided on behalf of central and local government bodies and other organizations, to assist the public in their dealings with such bodies; information about local clubs and societies, adult education facilities, sports organizations and places of entertainment.

1.16   Information for visitors to the area, including details of hotels, places to visit, and a diary of events.

Providing information

1.17   Accept responsibility for producing accurate up-to-date answers quickly, impartially, and – where appropriate – confidentially.

1.18   Be prepared if necessary to seek information outside the library's own resources, including other libraries, specialized agencies and unpublished sources.

1.19   Be prepared, in return, to handle enquiries referred by other agencies.

1.20   Train staff in branch libraries to act as information referral points for their localities, and ensure that central departments can handle their requests.

1.21   Publicize the information role of the public library through talks, printed publicity, local radio and television, and direct contacts with local bodies.

1.22   Offer instruction in the use of the library's information sources, and publish explanatory leaflets, including leaflets in minority languages. Prepare recordings on tapes, and in embossed type, for handicapped readers.

1.23   Provide an information board to carry public service information, and details of the aims and programmes of local organizations.

1.24   Take a lead in stimulating and coordinating local activities, and encourage organizations to contribute to a consolidated diary of local events.

1.25   Compile bibliographies and suggested reading lists on request.

1.26   Provide accommodation on library premises for other specialized community information services; coordinate the work of information and advice agencies throughtout the community.

1.27   Ensure that effective reference and information facilities are available at all times when the library is open.

1.28   Give advice on the use and understanding of sources, but not on their interpretation. When necessary, refer enquirers to appropriate specialists. Legal and medical information, in particular, should be given verbatim from published sources, without comment.

1.29   Place no restrictions on transmitting any information which is publicly available.

1.30   Provide a regular – perhaps weekly – "current awareness" service, indexing and/or abstracting new material in specific fields. Such a service might be directed particularly to official departments, institutions, industrial and commercial firms, and other organizations and individuals. Monitor its use to evaluate costs and benefits.

1.32   Accept enquiries by post or telephone, as well as by personal visit.

1.32   Provide computer terminals with which to obtain information from remote databanks, and use them whenever they will increase the efficiency of the service.

Charging for information in public libraries

1.33   The provision of information is an integral part of the public library's service. As such it should normally be provided without charge, though some restriction may have to be placed on the amount of staff time which can be devoted to an enquiry. (See para. 1.13). The fact that some information is now available not only from published documents but also from computerised databanks should not be allowed to undermine this general principle. To obtain access to such information by means of a terminal in a library is often quicker and more effective than familiar manual methods of searching. The costs, however, being more easily identifiable, may sometimes seem high, and some library authorities are known to take the view that they are unable or unwilling to introduce this facility if they are required to bear the full cost of its use.

1.34   IFLA's Working Group on the Impact of Technology on Public Libraries has argued that at the beginning of an era in which information will become more and more important for the individual and for society as a whole, it is not logical to propose restrictions on free access.* Any introduction of charges is bound to restrict access to some information to those who can afford to pay for it. It is also contrary to the public library tradition, to the spirit of the Unesco Public Library Manifesto, and to public library legislation in most enlightened countries.

1.35   The Working Group which has prepared these guidelines recognizes strong objections in principle to imposing any charges for access to information, and has been reluctant to appear to acquiesce in the

* _Impact of Information Technology upon Public Libraries._ Report of a Working Group under the IFLA Section of Public Libraries. 1984.

practice by discussing limitations which might be imposed on charges. Nevertheless, the following guidelines have been drawn up to assist any library authorities which feel obliged to choose between making a charge for access to computerised information, and failing to provide it:

1. No charge should be made unless use of the computerised service is specifically requested; use at the discretion of library staff should not be subject to payment.

2. Staff dealing with information inquiries should be free to use whatever sources seem, in their professional judgment, to be most appropriate.

3. The charge made should not exceed the cost of computer time used.

4. Requests for information by individuals should be distinguished from those received from firms and commercial agencies: the former should be exempted from charges for a specified minimum period – perhaps five minutes of computer time.

1.36   The practice of obtaining publications and information from other external sources to satisfy requests should not be subject to charges, though photocopies specifically requested for retention by the user may be charged for at normal commercial rates.

Information about the locality

1.37   Each public library needs to be a main research library and information centre on matters concerning its own locality.

1.38   Aim to preserve a comprehensive collection of printed material about the locality.

1.39   Maintain a subject index of local material, incorporating an index to local newspapers.

1.40   Maintain a pictorial record of the area, both past and present, and encourage the deposit of prints, photographs and other material of local topographical, biographical and sociological significance.

1.41   Maintain good liaison with any other institution concerned with the provision and preservation of local information and archives.

1.42   Sponsor or encourage a local history study group, and the publication of research studies about the locality.

1.43   Undertake publication, by the library, of bibliographical aids to local studies, and of material for students from the library's own collections.

Activities for children

Many of the foregoing points are relevant to all age-groups. However, a programme of activities specifically for children encourages them to feel that visiting the library is an enjoyable and interesting experience. It can also play a more positive part in stimulating intellectual and social development. A well-planned programme of activities will encourage the use of the books and other materials in the library, and hence the interests which these promote, and will supplement them by involving the children in creative activities of many kinds. The range of activities need be limited only by the imaginativeness of the staff and the resources available in the library and the community. The following are merely a few examples.

1.44   Arrange talks, stories, readings, practical activities, hobby evenings and competitions, all designed to encourage participation by the children and to stimulate exploration of the library's resources.

1.45   Invite talented and interested adults – preferably professional performers and craftsmen, or skilled amateurs – to display, demonstrate and talk about their own occupations or hobbies.

1.46   Build upon the children's own hobbies, sports, experiences and interests.

1.47   Stimulate the children's own talents and creativity by helping them to run their own clubs, and to write and produce their own plays and exhibitions.

1.48   Encourage even the youngest children to enjoy family visits to the library by providing toys and games as well as books and pictures.

1.49   Mount and display collections of children's work, including drawings, photographs, assessments of books they have read. Maintain close liaison with schools.

1.50   Ensure that children who come to the library receive a general introduction, appropriate to their age, to its arrangement and use. This will often be achieved through organized visits by school classes.

1.51   Encourage children to help in the running of their library.

Cultural and social provision

The public library is inevitably one of the major cultural and social centres within its community. The extent to which this role should be developed depends on five main considerations:

1.   What other facilities are available in the community? Wasteful duplication should be avoided – but duplication is not always wasteful.

2.   If facilities are needed, is the public library the most suitable place in which to provide them?

3.   Should the library itself sponsor a cultural or social programme, or should it encourage other organizations to make use of library accommodation?

4.   Are existing library premises adequate and suitable, or can they be extended as necessary to accommodate the facilities contemplated? (On the flexible use of space, see para. 4.14).

5.   Will there be any benefits to the library itself in being associated with the provision of additional cultural or social facilities?

The following are examples of cultural and social activities which have been, or might be, provided in public libraries. Though they may often be informal in character, they will be most effective if provided as part of an organized programme.

1.52   Exhibitions, lectures, films, concerts, recitals of music or poetry.

1.53   A club for old people, possibly including evenings of personal reminiscences which would be worth recording for the library's local collection.

1.54   Headquarters for a community services committee.

1.55   Rehearsal accommodation for local music groups.

1.56   Cultural presentations by ethnic minority groups, including women and children; occasional more ambitious multi-cultural festivals.

1.57   Publication parties for new books, particularly by local authors.

1.58   The opportunity for other groups in the community to hold meetings or other activities, public or private, in a room or hall suitably equipped and of appropriate size.

Services for handicapped and disadvantaged people

Readers suffering from physical handicaps or confined to residential institutions should be enabled as far as possible to make use of the full range of library services generally available. Meeting their special needs may require liaison with national and local organizations, and the provision of library facilities in their own homes or institutions. One major problem which faces many libraries is that of identifying those members of the community whose handicaps prevent them from making full use of the library service. This can be achieved through publicity, the help of other agencies which cater for their needs, and through the recommendation of friends. Services which might be provided by the public library include the following.

Housebound readers

1.59   Home delivery services, using either library transport or local volunteers. Such a service should be the responsibility of a professional librarian, who should personally undertake a proportion of the visits. Policy regarding loans to housebound readers should be generous: no strict limit to the number of books or other media which may be borrowed at one time, careful regard to individual needs and interests, and prompt attention to specific requests. Visits should be on a pre-arranged, regular basis, at intervals of 2–4 weeks.

1.60   From time to time special arrangements should be made, perhaps with the help of local organizations, to bring to the library many of the readers who are normally housebound. They can then see all that the library has to offer, and hence be better able to make good use of its services. Such visits also provide a change of scene, and a social gathering which can be made the occasion for a programme of library-based interest and entertainment.

Readers in hospitals, residential homes, day centres, prisons and correctional institutions

1.61   Services to hospitals and prisons should be provided by public libraries as an integral part of their service to the community.
Costs of administration, staff and materials, however, may be shared with the institution on an agreed basis. In hospitals, the public library may be responsible both for staff libraries and for services to patients, under the control of a single professional librarian or a coordinated team.

1.62   In all such institutions, the facilities provided should include the normal range of information and request services, and it will often be helpful to introduce people to their home libraries when they are discharged.

1.63   Public libraries which serve many institutions may need a special department for the purpose, with trained staff working both at headquarters and – by arrangement – within the institutions concerned.

1.64   Old people's homes, residential institutions and day centres are commonly served by unstaffed "deposit collections", exchanged regularly and supplemented by periodic visits from a mobile library with professional staff. Larger homes and institutions may need a trolley service to individual rooms.

Blind people and others with reading handicaps

1.65   There are many people in all countries who find it difficult or impossible to read a normal printed text as encountered in a book or newspaper.

They include dyslexics, aphasics, those who find page-turning difficult, and those who have never learned to read well. Public libraries have a responsibility to do their utmost to satisfy the needs of such people. They can often make good use of talking books and other audio material – though these are provided mainly for blind people – and of books and other printed materials which have been specially designed to make them easy to read.

1.66   Embossed literature and "talking books" are often made available to the blind through national organizations. In some cases the provision of talking books is assisted by public libraries through a system of decentralization. Elsewhere, the role of the public library may be to ensure that people are aware of the services available. or to act as local delivery points.

1.67   The range of talking books available is inevitably limited, and libraries can help by making special needs known to the relevant organizations and publishers.

1.68   Libraries can also make recordings themselves to meet urgent local demands, but copyright problems may sometimes have to be overcome before this can be done.

1.69   National and international news is widely available to blind people on radio, and sometimes by nationwide talking newspapers produced by libraries and organizations for the blind. A role more clearly suited to local public libraries is the production of a talking newspaper containing local news and information.

1.70   A selection of large-print books for the partially sighted is a normal part of public library provision.

1.71   Public libraries should cooperate in all possible ways with organizations providing tuition for sighted people who need training in literacy. Their main role is to ensure that suitable materials are available, and if necessary to provide convenient and congenial accommodation where tuition can take place.

1.72   Video-recordings for deaf people may be available from national agencies, or they may be provided by public libraries in the same way as talking books.

Services to ethnic and linguistic minorities

Ethnic and linguistic minorities may be unable to make full use of the public library services generally available. They are often unable to read the language of the community in which they are living, and many may be weak readers even in their own language. They also have additional needs as a result of their different cultural patterns and problems of harmonizing with the majority community. Many, also, are likely to be at a disadvantage socially and financially compared with the rest of the community. For all these reasons they need special services from the public library.

1.73 Public libraries should take positive steps to identify the needs and problems of ethnic and linguistic minorities in their own areas, provide requisite materials and services and encourage their use.

1.74 Central organizations with responsibility for libraries can assist by establishing liaison with relevant national bodies which represent the interests of minority groups.

1.75 Local leaders of minority groups should be approached to ensure their understanding of the libraries' services, and to enlist their cooperation in encouraging their use.

1.76 The employment, even part-time, of staff with appropriate linguistic abilities is very desirable.

1.77 Materials, including newspapers, in minority languages, often have to be obtained from their countries of origin. National organizations or specialist booksellers may be able to assist in this, or several library systems with similar needs may arrange to act collectively.

1.78 When several small minority communities have a need for printed or audiovisual materials in the same language, it will often be inefficient for each library to try to satisfy their needs individually, each with its own very limited range of material. Cooperative arrangements to circulate a wider range of material among the several library systems concerned may be more satisfactory. Alternatively, a national loan collection of such material might be established to supplement local holdings.

1.79 Information sheets in minority languages, describing the library services and other local facilities, need to be produced and distributed, mainly through the groups' own community organizations.
With encouragement and assistance from the library, these and other publications might be produced by members of the minority community themselves.

1.80 Children from minority groups face particular difficulties if they are to live happily within an alien community without losing their own cultural heritage. Libraries need to be aware of this danger, and provide adequate materials about the history and culture of the countries from which immigrant groups have come, and books and periodicals for children in their own languages.

1.81   Ethnic minorities can enrich the life of the communities in which they live by preserving their cultural traditions and continuing as far as possible to practise their own customs. The public library can assist in both these processes by promoting performances and exhibitions of traditional life and culture.

1.82   The majority group within each community may need help in understanding the different cultures and backgrounds of the minority groups in their midst. For these too the public library is a main source of information and guidance.

Services to schools

These guidelines are concerned with public libraries, not school libraries. (For the multi-purpose library, see para. 4.21). Each school needs its own library, which may rely for support either on the public library or on a separate organization. Whatever the situation, the public library will need to provide assistance both to individual teachers and to children.

1.83   A close working arrangement needs to be established between the public library and local schools, to ensure the best coordination of their resources.

1.84   When school libraries are weak, or non-existent, the public library may need to provide stronger support, including the loan of general reading collections and of material relevant to specific topics in the curriculum.

1.85   Children need to be introduced from an early age to the wider resources available to them through the public library. Class visits should be encouraged, preferably related to work currently being undertaken in school. A programme of several visits throughout school life will enable the children to become familiar with the extent, organization and use of the collections, at a level matching their own increasing needs and abilities.

Chapter 2

MEDIA OF COMMUNICATION

Public libraries cannot discharge their responsibilities solely by providing access to books and other printed materials. Although these remain the most numerous and obvious means of communication, they must be supplemented more and more by other audiovisual media, and by information sources to which access must be obtained by electronic means. In some fields indeed these may be more important than books. There need be no limit to the sources to which the public library may turn to meet the need for information: manuscript notes and the personal knowledge of experts may sometimes be more useful than published materials or computerised databanks. No materials other than those prohibited by law should be barred from inclusion in library collections, and a wide range of viewpoints should be offered on controversial issues.

This chapter will deal successively with printed books, periodicals, audiovisual materials, and computerised sources of information.

PRINTED BOOKS

The public library provides books and information for people of all ages and all interests. Some wish to find a selection of books which they can read for pleasure, or which will arouse their interest; some, with interest already aroused, seek books on specific subjects at a level suitable to their needs. Some have reading interests which they share with many thousands of others; some have more specialized needs, or wish to pursue their interests to a greater depth or in greater detail.

Collections for lending

2.1   A "balanced bookstock", including a comprehensive collection of standard works in all fields, the main literary classics, and representative publications in other main languages, should be the aim within any large library system, taken as a whole. The depth of coverage in each field should be related to potential demand within the area.

2.2   The main factor determining the scope of the bookstock in each individual library should be the balance of local tastes and interests: but the library's role in encouraging new interests and broadening horizons should not be overlooked.

2.3 Small service points cannot afford to carry stock which will occupy the shelves unused, but they should be able to demonstrate the full range of resources available.

2.4 For the browsers, the readers for pleasure, and those with interests of a popular kind, each service point should be able to provide a choice of relevant material, with something fresh at each visit.

2.5 When shelf stocks are small it is necessary to organize a regular movement of books from one library to another to ensure that the choice available to any one reader is constantly refreshed.

2.6 The reader with more specialized needs cannot reasonably expect to be satisfied consistently from the open shelf stock in a small service point, but staff can ensure that relevant books are made available.

2.7 Facilities should be available in all service points for readers to request specific titles, or books on specific subjects.

Open shelves and reserve stock

2.8 The bookstock within a library system will usually consist of the working stock on open shelves at each service point, and a "reserve" stock which may be housed centrally or distributed among larger libraries.

2.9 The working stock consists of books which are individually in demand, books on subjects of current or perennial interest, or books which demonstrate the breadth and depth of the library's resources.

2.10 The reserve stock consists mainly of older books still likely to be needed from time to time. It is usually accommodated in stack rooms closed to the public, though limited access may sometimes be permitted. In some countries libraries are encouraged to deposit little-used books in national or regional reserve collections, for the use of all. Any reserve stock is expensive to house and administer: it should not be allowed to expand regardless of potential value.

2.11 Efficient means of reference to, and withdrawal from, the reserve stock should be available to all service points in order that full value may be obtained from the investment which it represents.

2.12 Each service point is likely to build up its own small supplementary reserve collection, containing duplicate copies, books in seasonal demand, and others waiting to refresh the shelves. These collections should be kept to the minimum needed for convenient stock maintenance.

Reference books

2.13 All books in the library are assumed to be available for consultation on library premises. Some, however, need to be available for consultation at all times, and so cannot be loaned. Most of these are "quick reference" books whose contents are arranged in a systematic way to facilitate use. They include dictionaries, directories, atlases, and yearbooks of many kinds. Even the smallest service point is likely to need a few of these books to answer simple enquiries. Duplicate copies of some of them should be available for loan.

2.14 The size of the quick reference collection will increase with the size of the library. Although the collection should be intended to anticipate demand, the temptation to build up an unnecessarily comprehensive range of expensive publications should be resisted.

2.15 In addition to quick reference books, larger libraries need to provide a collection of standard works for reference and research use. The scope of this collection should be related to likely needs and demands and to other reference facilities available in the vicinity – for example, in university or college libraries, special libraries and information services.

Local studies

2.16 In this field public libraries commonly aim to provide comprehensive research collections. They include, and permanently conserve, published material relating to the locality, both past and present, in all media; local ephemera; and prints, photographs, maps and other local records.

Books for children

2.17 Children under fourteen years of age are likely to constitute at least 25–30% of the population, and can be expected to read more voraciously than adults. These factors need to be reflected in library collections.

2.18 The public library begins to serve children in their earliest years, by providing picture books or simple stories to be read aloud by parents or friends. This experience, enjoyable and valuable in itself, can profoundly influence the child's future attitude to books and reading.

2.19 Books provided for children should be produced to the highest standards of writing, illustration and production, thus encouraging an early appreciation of books themselves as well as of their contents.

2.20 Children, like adults, need to use reference books in connection with their studies and their other interests, and also to satisfy their natural curiosity. As they grow older, many of their needs will be best satisfied through access to the main (adult) reference collection, but there will be a need to provide simpler dictionaries, encyclopedias and other works specifically designed for younger children.

A CHECKLIST OF MATERIAL TO BE CONSIDERED FOR IN-CLUSION IN BOOK COLLECTIONS AT EACH SERVICE POINT

For adults

Non-fiction on all subjects of general or local interest, at different levels, and in proportions related to needs; simple guides and practical manuals, standard works and popular light reading; books to open minds and broaden horizons.

Selections of more specialized books related to the known interests of users but serving also to demonstrate the wealth of material available in the library system as a whole.

Imaginative literature: poetry, drama and fiction, including popular, standard and classical writings, and new and experimental work by young authors.

Representative works in the main world languages, and in minority languages used in the area served by the library.

Maps and guidebooks.

Special collections on the locality, and on commerce, technology, agriculture, etc., according to local needs.

National and international official publications.

Quick reference books in up-to-date editions, and other standard reference works.

Pamphlet collections: holiday guides, transport timetables, trade catalogues, etc.

Material to assist training in literacy.

Books for immigrant and ethnic minority groups, in their own languages and about their own countries and cultures.

Large print books for the partially sighted.

Embossed books for the blind (unless they are provided by other agencies).

Playsets for group reading.

Sheet music, and music in sets of orchestral parts.

For children

As for adults wherever relevant, but with the following special emphases:

Picture books and simple stories.

Imaginative literature for each age group, specifically designed to be attractive to children.

Factual books and simple discussion books, on all subjects and at various appropriate levels, attractively presented to arouse interest and encourage children to explore new fields.

Dictionaries, encyclopedias and other reference books designed especially for young people.

The management of book collections

2.21 Bookstocks need to be constantly refreshed. Bookfunds should be sufficient to allow the library system to acquire new purchases relevant to its objectives and to its users' needs.

2.22 Library users entering any service point should expect to find that about a quarter of the books on open shelves are less than five years old.

2.23 Older books need to be weeded out when they are physically worn out, out-of-date, or no longer of current interest. Good physical condition alone is not sufficient reason for keeping a book on a library's shelves. The useful life of some books may be extended by transferring them to other service points where they will find new readers.

2.24 In large libraries with a heavy volume of use, the average use per volume in any given period will be higher than in smaller and less well used service points. The proportion of funds required for stock replenishment will therefore tend to rise as a library becomes established and stocks grow.

2.25 In some developing countries in particular, home book production may not employ a high standard of paper and binding, and physical deterioration may be a very serious problem. This should be allowed for in the allocation of funds for the maintenance and development of bookstocks.

2.26 Books purchased in paper covers will have a longer life if they are bound or laminated before use. The cost of this must be justified by increased life-expectancy. Many books published in publishers' casings will need to be rebound later in their lives, before they become unusable. Regular review of the need for binding, and of the funds needed for this purpose, is therefore of the utmost importance.

2.27   Public libraries may sometimes become aware of, or may themselves generate, a need for certain books which are not currently available. On this, and on the quality of book production, librarians and their organizations can give knowledgeable advice to publishers.

2.28   In some circumstances library authorities or professional associations may themselves undertake publication to fill gaps in the materials available. For example, this may be appropriate when each service point of a large library system needs to have access to a similar compendium of local information.

2.29   Once acquired by the library, books need to be catalogued, displayed, and made accessible to users. The catalogues, which may be arranged by authors or subjects (or both), serve to identify the materials which are in stock and their location within the library system. Many countries provide a centralised service for the production of catalogue entries, possibly linked to a national bibliography. Within each library system the production of catalogues is also usually centralised, copies being made available throughout the system. It is important to be able to locate wanted books quickly, both within the library system and outside it. Simple means of transferring books from one service point to another without laborious recataloguing are also desirable.

2.30   Although many library catalogues are still on cards, all these problems are now most easily solved by the use of a computerised catalogue, which can be linked if required to a computerised issuing system. Such a catalogue is usually made available at service points on microfiche because of the cost and inconvenience of paper print-out. However, a computer catalogue "on-line", using a visual display unit with print-out only on demand, is likely before long to become the norm.

2.31   When the majority of users can be expected to be seeking particular books, or books on known subjects, strict adherance to systematic classified order on the shelves is desirable. There are advantages in securing the adoption of a common classification scheme within a single country.

2.32   In smaller service points, or in those sections of larger libraries where these conditions do not apply, a less formal grouping on the lines commonly adopted in bookshops, may be more helpful to users who have no pre-determined book or subject in mind. Broad subject displays which bring together related material – not necessarily books alone – from different parts of the library may be particularly helpful, especially when the subject is of topical interest.

PERIODICALS, INCLUDING NEWSPAPERS

2.33　Many periodicals are designed to be read, or looked at, for pleasure, and then discarded. If provided in public libraries they are unlikely to be retained permanently in stock. Such periodicals often contain well-written articles on topics of current interest, and these may sometimes be worth extracting and including in the library's information files.

2.34　A second group, containing material of greater substance, social content, and more permanent value, provides the pool from which most public library acquisitions are likely to be drawn. Many periodicals for ethnic minorities and other sections of the community with special interests are likely to be in this group. Files of back numbers are usually retained as long as they are in demand, or provide useful information sources.

2.35　A third group, mainly the journals of learned societies and other research bodies, retain permanent value. Although they may attract a relatively small group of subscribers and readers at the time of publication, they will subsequently be referred to in subject indexes and other articles and research papers, and will therefore be asked for by name from time to time in libraries. Periodicals of this kind at one time occupied a most important place in the stocks of public libraries. The extent of their provision has more recently been reduced by two factors: their increasing cost, and the greater ease with which it is now possible to obtain or borrow copies from national and specialized collections when they are specifically required.

2.36　In some countries the cost of subscriptions to newspapers and periodicals is considerable, and their management in libraries, involving acquisition, checking, indexing, displaying and filing, can be burdensome. However, periodicals contain current opinions and up-to-date news and information to supplement the book collection. Their value must be assessed carefully in regard both to current interest and to future research potential. In the case of newspapers, the importance of giving access to a variety of points of view needs to be given due consideration.

2.37　The binding of periodicals into volumes, even if they are intended to be retained for permanent reference use, is not usually to be recommended. Although binding offers some protection (particularly against the loss of individual issues) it makes transport and photocopying more difficult, and has the effect of putting a whole volume out of use whenever a single article is being consulted.

AUDIOVISUAL MATERIALS

2.38   Audiovisual materials in libraries include audio recordings (mainly discs and cassettes), slides, tape-slide programmes, filmstrips, filmloops, cine film, video recordings (mainly cassettes), computer software and overhead projector transparancies. (It is sometimes found convenient to include microforms, though these are usually reproductions of the printed word). Simple graphic and pictorial formats such as prints, photographs, posters and diagrams should also be included.

2.39   People nowadays are accustomed to aural and visual presentation. An ever-increasing amount of material is being produced in audiovisual formats, and these therefore form an increasingly important part of an integrated library service. They are particularly relevant for use with pre-school children, people in hospital, and those with reading problems of any kind, or difficulty in holding a book or turning a page.

2.40   In many instances audiovisual formats are more effective than their print-based counterparts. For example, movement is more readily understood if it is portrayed by moving images on film or videotape, sound recordings are indispensable for the enjoyment of music; foreign languages are more easily learned through the medium of sound recordings. In no circumstances should audiovisual materials be regarded as an additional luxury in library provision: they are necessary components in a fully integrated library service, complementary to the printed word.

2.41   The use of most audiovisual media requires special equipment, much of it dependent on the availability of electricity. In some countries this – and the difficulty of getting equipment serviced – may restrict use. Battery operated tape recorders and slide projectors however are widely available and could themselves be lent by the library.

2.42   Listening and viewing equipment of all relevant kinds needs to be provided in the library so that the materials can be used on library premises, tried out before they are borrowed, and checked by the staff on return. Group viewing and listening will usually be possible once equipment is available. The individual use of audio materials in the library requires the provision of headphones or soundproof booths. The provision of "workshop" facilities, where individuals can make their own audio and visual recordings, should not be overlooked.

2.43   Library staff should themselves make use of audio and visual recording equipment to build up local collections of dialect speech, customs, folksongs and reminiscences. Reference has been made elsewhere to the making of talking books and newspapers for the blind. In all these activities care must be taken not to infringe copyright regulations.

COMPUTERISED INFORMATION

2.44   In many countries computerised information sources are already accessible through at least the main public libraries. Teletex systems using television screens, which are available in some countries, may be operated directly by members of the public. Terminals giving on-line access to databanks also have a growing application in public libraries. The availability by such means of information which is not conveniently available in any other way will encourage their rapid proliferation in developed library systems.

2.45   Libraries have two roles in regard to computerised information: to provide access to information already available, and to contribute to the creation of new databanks, particular containing bibliographical and local service information.

2.46   The use of computer programmes in library housekeeping – for cataloguing and issue systems for example – has already been noted. Computer games and educational programmes can be a popular and instructive addition to library facilities for both adults and children.

Chapter 3

STAFFING

Public library services vary according to the needs of their communities and the resources available. Each library system and service point provides a unique combination of materials, equipment and services. Library staff need to be similarly varied in their personal qualities and qualifications. They may be broadly categorized as follows:

Professional librarians. Qualified by specialized education, usually at graduate or post-graduate level. Responsible for the planning and management of services to meet the needs of the community, the selection and administration of collections, assisting library users, and maintaining effective liaison between the library service and its community.

Clerical staff. Employed, both in offices and in public departments, on a wide range of tasks which do not call for professional qualifications in librarianship. Clerical staff however do need a variety of skills, and hence training courses of various kinds.

Manual staff. Mainly cleaners, porters, janitors and drivers.

In addition to these, large libraries may employ staff in other categories:

Other professionals concerned with the organization, conservation and exploitation of media of communication in particular fields. They may be subject specialists, or qualified for example as archivists or information scientists.

Administrators, many of whom are likely to be qualified librarians.

Technicians responsible for audiovisual or electronic materials and equipment, book-binders and repairers, display artists, etc.

Staff must be sufficient not only in total numbers but also in each of these categories. In particular, there must be sufficient professional librarians to carry out the tasks which require their training and skills.

Professional librarians

3.1 At least one professionally qualified librarian should be available in each service point or separate department where the volume of work justifies this, or where the service would otherwise fail to give maximum value to the community.

3.2 The volume and nature of the work in very small service points may not justify the presence of a professional librarian at all times, but these service points should at least be under the general supervision of a qualified librarian.

3.3 All clerical staff employed in public departments need to be fully aware, through their training, of the resources on which they can call, and should be able at short notice to seek information and advice from a qualified librarian.

3.4 The team of professional librarians within each library system should include specialists responsible for each of the main areas of service. When a specialist department – concerned for example with technical information or music – is well developed and well used, a team of such specialists may be needed, either concentrated at a central point or distributed among major libraries.

3.5 It is particularly important that library services to children should be the responsibility of specially trained librarians, and that all members of the staff engaged in general services to the public should be aware of the special needs of children and able to assist them in the library.

3.6 All specialists need to be able to contribute to the service as a whole, both within their own special fields and as members of management teams. Care must be taken that their responsibilities within special fields do not infringe those of librarians with overall responsibility for regional, district and branch libraries and for other areas of administration. To these, the specialist may act as adviser or consultant, the ultimate responsibility for the service remaining with the head of the library or department.

3.7 The public library should as a matter of course establish good relations with subject specialists of many kinds outside its own organization. Some of these may be in libraries elsewhere, others in other establishments or in private life. All are likely to be assisted in some way by the public library service, and many will be able and willing to help from time to time with their special knowledge and advice, if called upon informally to do so.

Numbers of staff

3.8 Many factors affect staff requirements in public libraries. They include the size and composition of the population served, the extent of its demands on the library, the range of services provided, the number of service points and the hours during which they remain open.

3.9 In the past, recommendations regarding staffing levels were related mainly to population, but such recommendations could provide no more than a basis for more refined assessments. It is self-evident that a well-developed service which is heavily used requires many more staff than a rudimentary service for the same population. Good service generates a high level of demand, and although it is therefore more costly to maintain it gives greater benefit to the community in return.

3.10 In any community there must be sufficient staff, in each category, to carry out the functions allocated to them with the resources at their disposal. Staff requirements on this basis need to be kept constantly under review. Valid conclusions can be drawn only from a process of scientific work measurement in which the factors noted above can be weighted according to local conditions. Comparison with strictly similar conditions elsewhere may provide useful guidance.

Part-time staff

3.11 There may often be a need to employ staff on a part-time basis. Even among some professional librarians part-time employment may have some attractions, and there are benefits to employers in the greater flexibility which it makes possible. More commonly, it is likely that the clerical staff in remote branch libraries, open for a few days each week, will be recruited locally and employed only for those limited hours of duty. Part-time clerical staff pose special training problems if they are to identify fully with the aims of the library, and be aware of its ramifications. Most, however, prove to be exceptionally loyal and enthusiastic.

3.12 Because of the difficulties involved in providing relief staff from elsewhere, it is desirable that every remote library should be able, at short notice, to call upon local people for casual part-time employment in the event of sickness or other unavoidable absence of permanent staff. Standby staff need to be identified, trained, and given some practical experience before it becomes necessary to ask them for assistance in an emergency.

Personal qualities of library staff

3.13 Work in a public library provides scope for many talents. Circumstances vary from country to country, but the skilled use of organized collections of information requires the ability to communicate with people, sympathize with their needs and inspire their confidence. This calls for an out-going personality and some of the skills of a social worker. To track down their references and elucidate their problems may require a good general knowledge and the mind of a scholar. Because most public libraries serve communities of mixed race, religion and cultural traditions, and play an important part in assisting their harmonious development, librarians need to be sympathetic to such a role, able to relate to people of different backgrounds, and positive in identifying and meeting their needs impartially.

Since public libraries nowadays offer wider services than the provision of books and information, the successful librarian will need flair, vision and imagination to anticipate community needs and identify opportunities for improving the library's contribution towards meeting them.

Education and qualifications

3.14 Educational standards demanded on recruitment must have regard to the current labour market. They should not be excessive in relation to the tasks to be performed. The division of work among the respective recruitment categories should relate to their qualifications and aspirations.

3.15 Professional education promotes an understanding of the role of libraries, and hence an ability to contribute to their development in response to perceived needs. It now customarily preceeds employment in a library. Most countries have their own schools of librarianship. If they do not, then intending professional librarians must obtain their professional education and qualifications elsewhere. After qualification, all professional staff need to keep in touch with developments by wide reading and by attending courses.

3.16 It is in the interests of employers and their chief librarians that they should maintain close liaison with schools of librarianship. In this way the schools will be better able to understand their ever-changing needs, and they themselves will remain aware of the aims and methods of professional education. Lecturers in schools of librarianship, and their students, need to be closely involved with current practices in public librarianship, and to have opportunities for practical experience in this field. The sympathetic cooperation of senior librarians will assist in this.

3.17 It will become increasingly recognized that non-professional staff also need to attend educational courses on the ever-changing role of the public library. These may necessitate absence from existing employment with the agreement of employers, in whose interest the courses are provided.

Training

3.18   Training is complementary to education. It enables staff to understand the working of a particular library system, and to carry out effectively a specific range of tasks within that system. In addition, retraining and refresher courses prepare experienced staff for new responsibilities, as practices change or in preparation for a change of post within the system.

3.19   Training, therefore, is a means, which no employer can afford to ignore, of sharpening the abilities and developing and retaining the interest of staff, and of ensuring the maximum value from their services.

3.20   The need for training applies both to professional and to non-professional staff. For the latter it may sometimes have to stand alone, without any background of theoretical education.

3.21   Training will often be carried out systematically within a single library authority, where it can provide a planned programme of staff development. Courses on matters of wider relevance, however, may also be provided in library schools and other educational institutions. Senior librarians and employing authorities will wish in their own interests to encourage and assist staff to attend these courses, as well as other meetings which help to increase professional competence and awareness.

3.22   In large library systems a specialist member of staff may be given general responsibility for personnel and training, including the organization of staff training programmes and liaison with schools of librarianship.

3.23   All members of the library staff, and especially those who work directly with the public, need to have a good knowledge of the whole of the library system and its services. For those whose work cuts them off from most of their colleagues – in small branch libraries for example – it is especially important to be able to deal confidently and competently with most problems as they arise, and to know where to apply if necessary for additional information or advice.

A CHECKLIST OF BACKGROUND INFORMATION
REQUIRED BY EVERY MEMBER OF THE STAFF

The objectives of the library service

The national library background

The local community and local government background

The function of his/her own branch or department, and its relevance to the service as a whole

The contribution which his/her own job makes to the service

The names and duties of other people in the same department, and of main contacts elsewhere

Conditions of employment: salary, hours, holidays, promotion and career prospects and the experience and qualifications which will be required at each stage

Staff management

3.24 The staff of a public library may be organized in a hierarchy, with clear lines of delegation, or in teams which have shared responsibility for particular aspects of the service. Each member needs to know his place in the system, and the extent of his own responsibilities. It is the task of management to provide a structure within which the maximum success and satisfaction can be achieved.

3.25 Within each community some allowance of staff time should be made for work outside the library, including assessment of needs and promotion of services.

A CHECKLIST: FIVE TOOLS OF
LIBRARY STAFF MANAGEMENT

1. A statement of the objectives of the service as a whole, and of each branch and department within it.

2. An organization chart showing responsibilities and relationships for all members of staff in each branch, department, team or working group.

3. A job description for each post, indicating in general terms the duties of the post and its relationship to others.

4. A staff manual, available to all staff members, giving clear instructions on matters of common concern. (This manual will need piecemeal revision from time to time. A more comprehensive review, possibly linked with a review of working procedures, might be undertaken at, say, ten-yearly intervals).

5. Timesheets and duty schedules prepared as necessary within each department.

3.26 In a public library system, as in any other organization, high staff morale can be assisted by good communication. All members of the staff need to know what is happening elsewhere in the organization, and they need to be able to contribute their own criticisms, ideas and suggestions, and thus become involved in the management process. They also need to establish good relations on a personal level with their fellow workers – all the more important when workplaces are in widely separated locations, as public library branches tend to be.

A CHECKLIST: AIDS TO GOOD COM-
MUNICATION AND STAFF MORALE

Staff manual

Noticeboards and news bulletins (for both administrative and social information)

Small staff teams, working in official time, appointed to make recommendations on specific problems or developments; to include staff drawn from all relevant levels, including both experienced specialists and inexperienced trainees

A representative management committee in each branch or department

Occasional (and well-prepared) meetings of the full staff on matters of wide concern

Periodic social events to bring staff together informally, probably organized by a staff association

An annual one-day meeting, or short residential course, for training and social purposes, to bring together part-time staff who are normally employed in isolated branch libraries

An annual one-day meeting between staff and members of the management board or committee, to engage in joint discussion, based on prepared papers, of aspects of library policy and practice.

A senior management team, willing to delegate responsibility and receptive to suggestions and constructive criticisms

Chapter 4

SERVICE POINTS

This chapter discusses in a general way some factors relevant to the provision of public library service points. The management of service points is further discussed in Chapter 5.

4.1 The number and distribution of service points within a library system are determined mainly by geographical considerations and the distribution of population. Large towns need libraries with a correspondingly large range of specialized services, some of which may be maintained for the system as a whole. Smaller towns and large villages will need smaller branch libraries, open for shorter hours and providing a more limited range of materials and services, designed to meet the general and special local needs of the area.

4.2 Smaller communities which do not justify a permanent library building may be served by trailer or caravan libraries, which can be towed to a site and left there for a day or two before being transferred to a different location. Possible alternatives to this, used in the same way, are container libraries (delivered by flat-bed lorry and having the advantage of greater spaciousness and a flat floor) and "roll-on, roll-off" libraries (in which only the shelf units, already stocked, are delivered by van into an existing multi-purpose community room). All these methods are most easily adopted when a group of small communities, fairly close together, are connected by well-made roads.

4.3 Mobile libraries are suitable for serving more scattered populations, or locations which need specialized facilities. In urban areas they can serve pockets of population which are isolated by main roads or railways, and new developing communities which will eventually need static branch libraries.

4.4 The following is suggested as an appropriate order of priorities when setting up service points in a newly-established or developing library system:

1. Provision of a headquarters as a base for planning and administration and for the development of supporting services.

2. Main (or "regional") libraries in major centres of population. Priority would be given to towns which might provide a service or an administrative centre for a wide area.

3. District libraries in medium-sized towns.

4. Branch libraries in small towns and large villages.

5. Mobile libraries and other services in rural areas.

6. Sub-branch libraries in larger towns.

4.5 When a pattern of service points is being developed in an urban area, two considerations must be carefully balanced: easy accessibility and depth of service.

4.6 A large number of small libraries can provide a basic service within a short distance of most potential users. Libraries of this kind, if well managed and with a constant circulation of stock, can meet adequately most needs for purely recreational reading and provide remote access to the full range of the library's services.

4.7 A smaller number of larger libraries could provide, for a similar cost, a service in greater depth for readers who would travel farther to use it. A well-equipped and amply stocked library of this kind cannot be provided close to every home. But most people travel from time to time to certain focal points in their communities, usually for shopping or entertainment, and libraries which are located in such places will be able to serve users from a wide area. The main consideration is the attractiveness of the focal centre as a whole, not that of the library alone. For maximum effect the library should be close to the main stream of pedestrian traffic, well served by public transport, and with adequate car parking space nearby.

4.8 New public library buildings should be so designed that they do not obstruct use by the infirm and the physically handicapped, and older buildings should wherever possible be modified to facilitate such use.

4.9 The value of a library can be measured only in terms of its service to the community. A central site in a main focal point may be twice as expensive as a fringe site; but site costs are a small proportion of total capital and running costs over the life of a building. If a library on such a site attracts more than twice the amount of use the higher cost has been well justified.

Layout and planning

4.10 It will usually be necessary to provide in each public library building lending and reference facilities for both adults and children, but the relative importance of these varies considerably in different circumstances. A decision about their range and extent must be made before space requirements can be determined.

4.11 The separation of children from adults, and lending materials from

44

reference materials, is customary in large libraries. In small and medium-sized libraries the degree of separation should be kept to a minimum, with easy access from one section to another. Children and parents should be able to enjoy the experience of choosing books together, and older children will often need access to books in the "adult" section of the library. Children however do need to have a library area which they can feel is their own, even if they invite adults to share it with them. Scale, style of decoration, and some attractive but unconventional furniture all help them to feel comfortable and at home.

4.12 The transition from childhood to adulthood has usually been assumed to occur at about the age of fourteen, but this is an arbitrary assumption. Some libraries now have separate children's departments only for children under eleven, enabling the staff to concentrate on their more clearly recognizable special needs. Any variation from the traditional pattern has implications for the numbers and training of staff, und for the space requirements and decor appropriate to the children's library.

4.13 It has not been customary to provide separate library departments for teenagers, and it is probably not desirable to do so. It is more helpful to assist their transition to adulthood than to emphasize their temporary separateness. The fact that young people between fourteen and twenty tend to drift away from using public libraries need not cause too much concern: it is important only that librarians should not drive them away by unimaginative selection policies and by a drab and unwelcoming atmosphere in the library as a whole. The attractive presentation of the library, both outside and in, is important for potential users of all ages.

4.14 All public library buildings should be planned to meet foreseeable future needs, preferably based on a projection of up to twenty years. If possible the site should allow for future expansion, and the building plan – including arrangements for heating, lighting and other technical services – should provide both for expansion and for the flexible use of space. Even in large libraries it will often be better to provide areas for different purposes rather than separate rooms or departments. An openplan building, giving maximum flexibility, may best meet this requirement.

4.15 The functions of a library building should be immediately apparent from outside. The location and design alone can achieve valuable publicity for the services which the library provides. It will often be possible to allow views into the building to enable passers-by to see its services in action. Exterior display cases and a well-planned entrance hall can be used to similar effect.

4.16 A public library should be kept open for as long, and at such times, as the need justifies. In a main city library this is likely to be at least sixty hours a week. Each library building represents a considerable investment of the community's resources, and must be used as fully as possible for purposes which benefit the community. This includes use outside library opening hours, and purposes which may sometimes lie outside a narrow interpretation of the library's function.

A public library as part of a larger complex

4.17   There are many reasons why a public library might be built as part of a larger complex of public buildings. The arrangement may sometimes benefit the providing authority (economy, availability of a site, convenience of unified management of the building), but it may sometimes be to the advantage of the library and the community as a whole. In all cases the suitability of the site for library purposes should be a paramount consideration, and the location of the library within the complex – normally on the ground floor – should be chosen with full appreciation of the importance of visibility, and the large number of daily visits which can be expected. Complexes of three kinds are identified below.

4.18   *Association with related services.* Libraries, museums, and cultural centres of other kinds have overlapping interests and many users in common. Each can benefit from a close physical relationship, and there have been many cases of successful joint management.

4.19   *Groupings which have the effect of extending the use of the library.* The public library is more easily accessible to the staff and users of any other service with which it shares accommodation. Moreover, two services together may justify additional facilities, such as a refreshment counter or a lecture room, which one alone could not always support. A "community centre", which provides accommodation for a variety of local activities and hence draws in groups with many different interests, might be a particularly suitable partner for a public library. However, a swimming pool, a health centre, and a doctor's waiting room have all been known to share site or premises with a public library with some advantage on both sides. In any joint arrangement of this kind it is important that the separate identity of the public library should be carefully preserved: the library's main function is to provide access to information and to the media of communication, and no added functions, however desirable in themselves, should be allowed to blur or hinder the discharge of this responsibility.

4.20   *The multi-purpose library.* Each school and college needs its own library, but experience has shown that with careful planning and good management it is often possible for a public library located in the same building to fill that role without detriment to its wider public service. No

46

significant financial savings can be expected from such an arrangement, but worthwhile benefits in service can be achieved. The main criteria for success are as follows:

1. The location of the library, both within the community and within the building, must be satisfactory for all its functions.

2. The design of the library must permit use by the general public and by the school or college simultaneously. Alcoves and shielded areas are necessary for group working.

3. Arrangements for financing and management must be satisfactory to both sides: firm but flexible, with a clear allocation of responsibilities.

4. The librarian must have time to play a full part as librarian of the school or college, as well as carrying out a full range of duties to the public.

Chapter 5

THE MANAGEMENT OF PUBLIC LIBRARIES

A summary of desiderata for the establishment and management of public libraries is contained in the Unesco Public Library Manifesto (see Appendix I). It includes the requirement that the provision of public libraries should be required by law, and in most countries this is the case. Responsibility for public libraries, as for all services provided from public funds, lies with the central or local government authorities which are the main providers of those funds.

Management arrangements vary widely. A committee may be appointed with specific responsibility for the library service; or the public library may be one of several responsibilities of a larger and more powerful committee. The library service itself may form part of a complex of services, perhaps concerned with cultural or educational matters, under unified administrative control.

5.1   Whatever management structure is adopted, the professional librarian at the head of the public library service should have direct access to the board or committee which is directly responsible for the service.

5.2   The commonly understood objectives of public libraries (see page 8) provide a basis for formulating more detailed objectives for each library system. These will be consistent with the general objectives of public libraries, but will reflect specific local circumstances and perceived needs.

5.3   The adoption of these objectives by the managing body must be understood to imply an assurance of continuing financial commitment, making possible the provision of service points, staff, stock and equipment ("input") to support an agreed programme of developing services.

5.4   Although the public library service will be mainly supported from public funds, there need be no objection to accepting grants, gifts or sponsorship from non-public sources, provided that no conditions are attached which damage the normal concept and conduct of the public library service.

5.5   Subsequent processes in the management of a public library system are the same as those in the management of any comparable organization. They follow an annual cycle:

1. Review of needs.

2. Identification of priorities and immediate goals. (If there is not enough money to do everything well, it is better to select priorities than to do everything badly.)

3. Agreement as to the most effective strategies for achieving goals.

4. Budgeting: estimating the resources needed during the ensuing development period, leading to the allocation of funds.

5. Deployment of resources to achieve maximum performance.

6. Measurement of input and performance ("output") on a consistent and comparative basis.

7. Evaluation of performance in relation to input and other comparative measures.

8. Re-assessment of needs and policies.

The administrative unit (See Definitions)

5.6   Public libraries are usually the responsibility of multi-purpose units of local government. The size of these units is not likely to be related specifically to the needs of library administration, though there may sometimes be a choice between allocating library responsibilities to a larger or smaller tier of local government units. A low density of population, and hence large distances between service points, may make it desirable to have small administrative units, or a federal system of administration. On the other hand it is likely that limited economic resources can be deployed most effectively if coordinated over a large area. A relatively small administrative unit may enable a library service to relate closely to local needs; but the greater resources of a larger unit make possible the provision of specialized staff and services which would be uneconomical in a smaller unit.

5.7   When all relevant factors have been taken into consideration, it is likely that the largest available administrative units will be the ones best able to provide comprehensive and efficient library services.

5.8   Cooperation between library systems is necessary at all levels if the best possible services are to be provided. The librarian in a small administrative unit faces a particularly urgent need to establish cooperative arrangements with other library systems in order to enlarge the resources available to him. For the librarian in a large administrative unit the main challenge is to develop local contacts within each regional, district, or branch library area, in order to minimise the remoteness of his central administration.

5.9   Although developed countries have usually related their public library services to units of local government, a coordinated system organized on a national basis could be equally effective in a small country. It might also be especially appropriate in developing countries where the situation is not complicated by existing institutions, and where it is particularly important to ensure the most effective use of limited resources over a wide area.

The public library system as a network

5.10   The concept underlying a "public library system" is that no single service point should stand alone: each must be able to draw on the support of the system as a whole, and each should be able to provide access to the full resources of the system. Library users should be encouraged to regard their local service points in this way, and the staff and equipment of the service point should be such as to reinforce such a view.

5.11   The network efficiency of a public library system can be assessed by asking questions such as these:

1. How will the staff at a small branch library deal with a request for a specific book not in stock, or for a specific piece of information?

2. How quickly can such a request reach the librarian best able to deal with it?

3. How quickly can an answer be provided?

4. How efficient, in theory and in practice, are arrangements for locating within the system books and information requested, and delivering them to the enquirers?

5. Are the staff trained, and expected, to use the quickest means possible of satisfying requests?

6. Is the library's equipment – telephones, catalogues, bibliographies, printed forms, staff manuals, directories of specialized staff, inter-library transport, copying machines, computer terminals – adequate for its purpose?

7. Are the library's methods tested by periodic checks on delivery times, etc.?

5.12   For purposes of supervision and training, and the effective sharing of resources in a large system, it will often be found convenient to organize service points in a hierarchy, with branch libraries dependent to some extent on larger "district" libraries, district libraries on "regional" libraries in the main population centres, and these possibly on a main or central library. Administrative offices for the service as a whole may be located in the central library, or in separate accommodation elsewhere.

5.13 Senior specialist members of staff will usually be based at the central library or one of the regional libraries. Administrative arrangements, however, must ensure that their special abilities are made available throughout the system.
(Staff Management is further discussed in Chapter 3)

Management information

5.14 Within each library system, information must be gathered so that performance and progress can be evaluated. The basis of evaluation must inevitably be comparison – with goals, with last year's performance, with the performances of other similar library systems or of other service points within the same system. The collection and analysis of input and output statistics need not be costly, especially if the library's records are computerised. Its value lies in helping to identify effective policies and to eliminate future waste.

5.15 Performance statistics however do not provide answers. They merely make it possible to ask pertinent questions: why has library use increased or declined? Why is one library apparently more expensive than another?

5.16 In addition to the regular monthly, quarterly and/or annual analysis of input/output data, it is helpful to make periodic assessments of specific aspects of performance, such as the up-to-dateness of the shelf-stock, adequacy of subject coverage, and speed with which requests are satisfied.

5.17 The body responsible for providing the library service does not necessarily consist of library users. Other means may therefore have to be found – in addition to the collection and analysis of input and output statistics – to determine the extent to which the service satisfies their needs. The unexpressed needs of non-users must also be considered. It may be useful to establish local advisory committees in each library district, and to commission market surveys.

5.18 Management information, when collected, must be used. (All too often, collection is deemed to be an end in itself!) The conclusions which are drawn, when necessary correlations have been made, become part of the data on which the next cycle of management decisions will be based.

Chapter 6

NETWORKS AND SUPPORT SERVICES

The amount of recorded information and other published material grows steadily greater. Demand for efficient access increases world-wide and the need for it becomes more urgent: ready access to up-to-date information is recognized as a major key to the improvement of prosperity and the quality of life. No single library can expect to meet all the expressed and potential needs of its users. Public library systems, even when organized as efficient networks (see Chapter 5) cannot satisfy from their own resources all the demands for highly specialized materials which can arise in any community. These are often best met by pooling the resources of many libraries, or from national and specialized collections. Technological advances are making it easier to obtain records and information from remote locations by means of photocopiers, microforms, telecommunications and computers.

To provide efficiently for universal access to publications and information can be expensive. The degree of success is bound to be affected by economic constraints. It is important therefore to achieve maximum benefits at every level of provision: by efficient networking within a single library system, by inter-library cooperation, and by the provision of national support services.

A network among a group of libraries

6.1 It is in the interests of libraries of all kinds to participate in formal or informal networks for mutual support. Since the creation and efficient maintenance of a network makes demands on the participating organizations, searching questions need to be asked and answered before even a pilot scheme is undertaken: a network will only be successful if it is seen to confer benefits on users and members which could not be satisfactorily achieved in any other way.

6.2 A first requirement is that there should be a framework within which cooperation can take place: periodic meetings of librarians from different library systems, for example, provide a forum in which problems and possible solutions can be discussed. In many countries the national professional association establishes local groups of this kind; alternatively, senior librarians may make their own less formal arrangements.

6.3 Public library systems may benefit from cooperation with other public library systems, but there may be greater advantages in establishing

53

networks which also involve university, college and specialized technical and research libraries, whose resources are more likely to complement, rather than overlap, those of public libraries.

6.4   The main purpose of cooperative networks is likely to be the provision of access to a wider range of books and other materials. But there are other possible benefits, including the pooling of staff expertise and participation in joint projects such as publications, and the computerised cataloguing and location of materials.

6.5   *Cooperation,* in which each institution retains full autonomy, may sometimes be extended to *coordination,* in which group decisions are taken on such matters as responsibility for specific purchases or for developing subject collections. Participating libraries may sometimes need to enter into binding financial agreements to make coordination on these lines possible.

6.6   A public library system usually covers an area which contains several libraries of other kinds, and other agencies offering advice and information services. For this reason the librarian of the public library may be the most appropriate person to initiate any cooperative action.

6.7   Cooperative arrangements can most easily be established between equal partners, where each may expect both to contribute and to benefit. Some large or well-endowed library systems, however, may anticipate little benefit from participation in such arrangements, though their contribution could be vital to other members. For them, it may be necessary to institute compensatory payments, preferably in the form of government grants, though a subscription based on use might be devised within the network.

6.8   Although cooperative networks are most likely to be established among a group of neighbouring library systems, there are other valuable forms of networking which might usefully be established among more scattered systems which share similar problems, objectives or equipment. Modern computer and telecommunications techniques remove any necessity for geographical constraints.

National support services

6.9   Many of the facilities which individual library systems need to supplement their own resources might be provided more effectively by national agencies than by cooperative arrangements. They include:

1. Planning of the infrastructure for library and information services

2. Maintenance and publication of a national bibliography

3. Provision of central cataloguing facilities

4. A centre for library research and methodology

5. Advisory and consultation services

6. Supportive loan collections of books, periodicals, and other media

7. Planned development of computer data-bases

8. Central organization for design and production of furniture, equipment, stationary and other services.

9. Publishing, bookbinding and publicity

6.10   The initiative in establishing such facilities may be taken by governments or national institutions, by individual institutions or commercial bodies seeking to provide common services, or by professional bodies or groups of institutions which recognize a common need. Libraries and librarians, individually or through their collective bodies, can make an important contribution by arguing the case, whenever they see one, for centralised services for the benefit of all.

APPENDIX I

THE UNESCO PUBLIC LIBRARY MANIFESTO

The Manifesto is reproduced here in the form in which it was last issued, in 1972. It still provides a useful statement about the place of the public library in the community. Sections have been numbered to assist reference. References to the main report have been added wherever necessary to draw attention to changes of emphasis since 1972.

Unesco and public libraries

1. The United Nations Educational, Scientific and Cultural Organization was founded to promote peace and spiritual welfare by working through the minds of men and women.

2. This manifesto proclaims Unesco's belief in the public library as a living force for education, culture and information, and as an essential agent for the fostering of peace and understanding between people and between nations.

The public library

A democratic institution for education, culture, and information

3. The public library is a practical demonstration of democracy's faith in universal education as a continuing and lifelong process, in the appreciation of the achievement of humanity in knowledge and culture.

4. The public library is the principal means whereby the record of man's thoughts and ideas, and the expression of his creative imagination, are made freely available to all.

5. The public library is concerned with the refreshment of man's spirit by the provision of books for relaxation and pleasure, with assistance to the student, and with provision of up-to-date technical, scientific and sociological information.

6. The public library should be established under the clear mandate of law, so framed as to ensure nationwide provision of public library service. Organized co-operation between libraries is essential so that total national resources should be fully used and be at the service of any reader.

7. It should be maintained wholly from public funds, and no direct charge should be made to anyone for its services. (See 1.13, 1.33–35, 5.4)

8. To fulfil its purposes, the public library must be readily accessible, and its doors open for free and equal use by all members of the community regardless of race, colour, nationality, age, sex, religion, language, status or educational attainment.

Resources and services

9. The public library must offer to adults and children the opportunity to keep in touch with their times, to educate themselves continously and keep abreast of progress in the sciences and arts.

10. Its contents should be a living demonstration of the evolution of knowledge and culture, constantly reviewed, kept up to date and attractively presented. In this way it will help people form their own opinions and develop their creative and critical capacities and powers of appreciation. The public library is concerned with the communication of information and ideas, whatever the form in which these may be expressed.

11. Since the printed word has been for centuries the accepted medium for the communication of knowledge, ideas and information, books, periodicals, newspapers remain the most important resources of public libraries.

12. But science has created new forms of record and these will become an increasing part of the public library's stock, including print in reduced form for compact storage and transport, films, slides, gramophone records, audio and video tape, for adults and children, with the necessary equipment for individual use and for cultural activities.

13. The total collection should include material on all subjects, to satisfy all tastes at differing educational and cultural standards.

14. All languages used by a community should be represented, and there should be books of world importance in their original languages.

15. The public library building should be centrally situated, accessible to the physically handicapped, and open at times convenient to the user. The building and its furnishing should be attractive, informal and welcoming, and direct access by readers to the shelves is essential. (See 4.8)

16. The public library is a natural cultural centre for the community, bringing together as it does people of similar interests. Space and equipment are therefore necessary for exhibitions, discussions, lectures, musical performances and films, both for adults and children.

17. Branch libraries and mobile libraries should be provided in rural and suburban areas.

18. Trained and competent staff in adequate numbers are vital to select and organize resources and assist users. Special training will be required for many activities such as work with children and handicapped, audio-visual materials, and the organization of cultural activities.

Use by children

19. It is in early life that a taste for books and the habit of using libraries and their resources are most easily acquired. The public library has therefore a particular duty to provide opportunity for the informal and individual choice of books and other material by children. Special collections and, if possible, separate areas should be provided for them. The children's library can then become a lively, stimulating place, in which activities of various kinds will be a source of cultural inspiration. (See 4.11)

Use by students

20. Students of all ages must be able to rely on the public library to supplement the facilities provided by their academic institutions. Those pursuing individual studies may be entirely dependent on the public library to meet their needs for books and information.

The handicapped reader

21. There is an increasing concern with the welfare of the elderly and all handicapped people. Problems of loneliness, and mental and physical handicaps of all kinds, can be alleviated in many ways by the public library. (See 1.59–72)

22. Improved means of access, provision of mechanical reading aids, books in large print and recorded on tape, service in hospitals and institutions, and personal service to the home are some of the ways in which the public library can extend its services to those who need it most.

The public library in the community

23. The public library should be active and positive in its outlook, demonstrating the value of its services and encouraging their use.

24. It should link itself with other educational, social and cultural institutions, including schools, adult-education groups, leisure-activity groups and with those concerned with the promotion of the arts.

25. It should be watchful for the emergence of new needs and interests in the community, such as the establishment of groups with special reading requirements and new leisure interests to be represented in the library's collections and activities.

APPENDIX II

IFLA STANDARDS FOR PUBLIC LIBRARIES 1973/1977

The following are the quantitative recommendations contained in the 1973/ 1977 editions of the IFLA *Standards for Public Libraries.* They are summarized here for information only. The present volume of guidelines does not include quantitative recommendations, and argues – in the Introduction – that in the present state of library development they are not likely to be universally relevant. The figures in this appendix have not been revised since they were first published in 1973. They are usually intended to be minima. For details, please refer to the published volume.

PUBLIC LIBRARY SYSTEM

Preferred minimum population	150,000
Minimum population normally regarded as viable	50,000

ADMINISTRATIVE UNIT

Minimum population in any circumstances	3,000

SERVICE POINTS: OPENING HOURS

Urban main libraries	60 hours per week
Branch libraries	18–60 hours per week

BOOKSTOCKS

Minimum working stock for all departments, excluding special collections, calculated in relation to literate population:

In smallest administrative unit	3 volumes per inhabitant
In general circumstances	2 volumes per inhabitant

When children up to 14 years of age constitute 25–30% of the population, children's books should comprise one third of the total stock

Reference books (included above):

In smallest administrative unit	100 volumes
In general circumstances	Up to 10% of total stock

(Higher in very large administrative units)

Deposit collections:

When collections of books are deposited, often without staff supervision, for use in small communities, there should be at least four changes of stock annually, at least 200 volumes being changed on each occasion.

Annual additions per 1000 population:

In general circumstances	250 per annum
In small administrative units	300 per annum

Children's books in same proportion as in total stock (see above)

Reference books in libraries serving populations over 50,000   10% of all additions

PERIODICALS, INCLUDING NEWSPAPERS

In administrative units of up to 5000 population   50

In administrative units of 5000–100,000 population
10 per 1000 population

(These figures include multiple copies, periodicals in foreign languages, and periodicals for children).

GRAMOPHONE RECORDS AND TAPED RECORDINGS OF ALL KINDS (for populations up to 20,000)

Stock for use within the library	2000
Annual additions to maintain such a collection	300

Records for home use: no recommendation

COLLECTIONS FOR NATIONAL MINORITIES AND NON-INDIGENOUS GROUPS

Books in their own languages:

For groups of less than 500	100
For groups of 500–2000	1 book for 5 people
For populations over 2000	1 book for 10 people

Annual additions:

For groups up to 2000	1 book for 25 people
For populations over 2000	1 book for 50 people

Periodicals, including newspapers in their own languages
1 per 500 people

STAFF

Total non-manual staff (professional, clerical, administrative):

In smallest administrative unit
1 full-time qualified librarian with clerical assistance

In larger administrative units with developed library services
1 per 2000 population

In very large administrative units 1 per 2500 population

Qualified librarians:

In a developed, urban, compact unit 33% of total staff

In a library system with many branches and small service points
40% of total staff

(In a large library system one third of professional librarians should be specialized in children's work).

BUILDINGS

Distribution in urban areas:

A branch library within 1.5 km. (1 mile) of most residents.

A relatively large library within 3–4 km. (2–2.5 miles) of most residents.

Areas of departments, etc.:

Adult lending and reference facilities: see accompanying table.

Storage of reserve stock:

In closed access stacks allow 5.5m^2 (59 sq.ft.) per 1000 volumes. (This capacity will be approximately doubled if compact shelving is employed).

In limited access stacks allow 7m^2(75 sq.ft.) per 1000 volumes.

Display and consultation of newspapers and periodicals:

In libraries serving populations up to 20,000:1 seat per 2000 population.

For populations above 20,000:1 seat per 3000 population.

(Note however that local needs may vary widely. Allow 3 m^2(32 sq.ft.) per seat).

Storage and use of audiovisual materials: no standard recommended.

Areas for children:

Lending services: 16m^2(172 sq.ft.) for every 1000 volumes on open shelves. (This assumes that shelf units will be 4 shelves high).

Provision on this scale will allow for circulation space, staff counters, catalogues, etc.

The total area needed for lending purpose on the above basis is likely to be as follows:

In libraries serving populations up to 10,000: 75–100m^2(807–1076 sq.ft.)

In libraries serving populations between 10,000 and 20,000: 100–200m^2 (1076–2152 sq.ft.)

Study space: no standard recommended.

Children's activities:
If children are to be an audience: 1.5m^2(16 sq.ft.) per place.
For a variety of creative activities: 3m^2(32 sq.ft.) per place.

POPULATION SERVED	ADULT LENDING FACILITIES Open shelf accommodation			ADULT REFERENCE FACILITIES Open shelf accommodation		Seating area	
	Volumes per 1000 population	Total shelf capacity required	Floor area needed at 15m² per 1000 volumes (minimum 100 m²)	Number of volumes	Floor area needed at 10 m² per 1000 vols.	Number of places at 1.5 per 1000 pop.*	Floor area at 2.5 m² per place
3,000	1,333	4,000	100m² (1076sq.ft.)	100	1m² (11sq.ft)	5	13m² (140sq.ft.)
5,000	800	4,000	100m² 1076sq.ft.)	300	3m² (32sq.ft.)	8	20m² (215sq.ft.)
10,000	600	6,000	100m² (1076sq.ft.)	900	9m² (97sq.ft.)	15	38m² (410sq.ft.)
20,000	600	12,000	180m² (1938sq.ft.)	3,000	30m² (323sq.ft.)	30	75m² (807sq.ft.)
40,000	600	24,000	360m² (3875sq.ft.)	7,000	70m² (753sq.ft.)	60	150m² (1614sq.ft.)
60,000	600	36,000	540m² (5813sq.ft.)	12,000	120m² (1292sq.ft.)	75	188m² (2024sq.ft.)
80,000	550	44,000	660m² (7104sq.ft.)	16,000	160m² (1722sq.ft.)	120	300m² (3228sq.ft.)
100,000	500	50,000	750m² (8073sq.ft.)	20,000	200m² (2153sq.ft.)	150	375m² (4035sq.ft.)

* This level of provision can sometimes be reduced in libraries serving populations larger than 100,000.

NOTE. The above figures include circulation space, staff counters, catalogues, etc. They do not include provision for periodicals and audiovisual materials, which are referred to separately.

Staff accommodation:
Workrooms and offices: add 20% to the total area of public departments. (This will be equivalent to about 10–12m^2(108–129 sq.ft.) per staff member.

Rest rooms, kitchen, toilets, cloakrooms, etc.:

Number of staff	Total area required
2	8m^2 (86 sq.ft.)
10	40m^2 (431 sq.ft.)
20	60m^2 (646 sq.ft.)
50	120m^2 (1292 sq.ft.)
100	220m^2 (2368 sq.ft.)
200	400m^2 (4306 sq.ft.)

Circulation space or "balance area":

Circulation space consists of entrance hall, stairwells, lavatories, cloakrooms, lobbies and corridors outside the areas already discussed.

Allow 10–15% of all public areas and 20–25% of all staff areas. The higher figures are unlikely to be needed except in some large libraries. The lower figures (10% and 20% respectively) should be regarded as "balance area", available for any desired purpose within the building if careful planning has made it unnecessary to provide circulation space on this scale.

APPENDIX III

STATISTICS OF SELECTED LIBRARY SYSTEMS

Information was requested from a small sample of library systems – three in each of fifteen countries. The working group is grateful to colleagues in those countries who undertook to collect the information, and to the librarians who responded to their requests.

These are not necessarily the best provided or most heavily used systems in their respective countries, but they are likely to be above the average in these respects. Each was asked to provide the information listed on the next page, in relation to the year 1983 or 1983/84.

The answers which follow reveal the great variety in the provision and use of public libraries world-wide, and demonstrate the difficulty of formulating quantitative standards which will be relevant in all circumstances. Librarians who plan to make use of the guidelines in this volume may find it helpful to examine the figures in these tables, noting particularly those library systems whose circumstances appear similar to their own.

KEY TO STATISTICAL TABLES
  1. Country
  2. Library authority
  3. Area (hectares)
  4. Population
  5. Population per hectare

SERVICE POINTS

  6. Libraries with annual issues over 200,000
  7. Libraries with annual issues 100–200,000
  8. Libraries with annual issues 25–100,000
  9. Libraries with annual issues below 25,000
 10. Total number of static libraries
 11. Number of mobile libraries/book buses
 12. Libraries or collections in hospitals, etc.
 13. Does the public library service provide or contribute to the library service in schools?

EQUIPMENT AND TECHNOLOGICAL SERVICES

14. How many photocopying machines?
15. How many microfilm/fiche readers?
16. How many remote computer terminals?
17. Is there a computerised issue system?
18. If so, how many libraries are included?
19. Is there a computerised catalogue?

STAFF

How many paid staff in each category:
20. Professional librarians
21. Staff with other professional qualifications
22. Non-manual staff with no professional qualifications?
23. Drivers, janitors, porters, cleaners
24. Total paid staff

PRINTED AND OTHER MATERIALS IN STOCK

25. Books for adults
26. Books for children
27. Total books
28. Total books per 1000 population
29. Books added to stock last year
30. Newspapers and periodicals: titles
31. Sound recordings: number of discs, cassettes, etc.
32. Films and video-cassettes
33. Slides/transparencies: number of sets
34. Slides/transparencies: single slides not in sets
35. Microfilm/fiche: number of titles (not library catalogues)
36. Computer software: number of discs, cassettes, etc.

NUMBER OF LOANS LAST YEAR

37. Books for adults
38. Books for children
39. Total books
40. Total books per 1000 population
41. Sound recordings

1. AUSTRALIA

2.	Riverina New. S. Wales	Eastern Reg. Melbourne, Vic.	Burnside S. Australia
3.	1,926,300	2,844,980	
4.	81,850	225,810	30,000
5.	0,04	0,08	

SERVICE POINTS

6.	1	3	1
7.	–	3	–
8.	2	1	–
9.	5	–	–
10.	8	7	1
11.	1	3	2
12.	?	–	–
13.	No	Yes	No

EQUIPMENT AND TECHNOLOGICAL SERVICES

14.	1	10	2
15.	11	25	1
16.	–	1	–
17.	Yes	Yes	Yes
18.	8	7	1
19.	Yes	Yes	Yes

STAFF

20.	4	24.8	4
21.	1	11.5	1
22.	15.5	38.2	14
23.	0.4	–	–
24.	20.9	74.5	19

PRINTED AND OTHER MATERIALS IN STOCK

25.	95,725	204,976	63,000
26.	39,468	111,781	27,000
27.	135,193	316,757	90,000

28.	1,654	1,403	3,000
29.	7,000	22,313	13,000
30.	192	500	140
31.	2,100	2,428	4,400
32.	–	–	–
33.	–	–	–
34.	–	–	–
35.	20	–	–
36.	–	–	–

NUMBER OF LOANS LAST YEAR

37.	354,776	1,123,427	–
38.	54,990	407,409	–
39.	409,766	1,539,836	553,083
40.	5,006	6,819	18,436
41.	6,001	7,253	38,997

1. BRAZIL

2.	Joinville Sta Catarina	Salvador Bahia	São Paulo
3.	118,300		151,600
4.	235,812	1,506,602	9,210,021
5.	1,99		60,7

SERVICE POINTS

6.	–	–	
7.	–	–	
8.	–	–	
9.	3	4	
10.	3	4	53
11.	–	11	1
12.	1	13	64
13.	No	No	Yes

EQUIPMENT AND TECHNOLOGICAL SERVICES

14.	1	–	12
15.	–	1	5
16.	–	–	16
17.	No	No	No
18.	–	–	–
19.	No	No	Yes

STAFF

20.	2	76	292
21.	9	4	134
22.	3	103	665
23.	3	37	119
24.	17	220	1.210

PRINTED AND OTHER MATERIALS IN STOCK

25.	57,792	146,180	881,564
26.	4,468	19,343	488,257
27.	62,260	165,523	1,369,821

28.	264	109	149
29.	4,420	12,705	29,573
30.	–	1,382	993
31.	–	2,147	41,193
32.	–	374	9
33.	–	12	551
34.	–	1,287	46,795
35.	–	10	25
36.	–	–	–

NUMBER OF LOANS LAST YEAR

37.	49,726		462,867
38.	3,344		328,544
39.	53,080	33,111	791,411
40.	225	22	86
41.	–	–	–

1.DENMARK

2.	Graested-Gilleleje	Kolding	Århus
3.	13,419	23,856	46,883
4.	15,700	56,435	248,688
5.	1.2	2.4	5.3

SERVICE POINTS

6.	1	1	6
7.	–	–	5
8.	2	1	17
9.	2	–	4
10.	5	2	32
11.	–	1	1
12.	1	2	39
13.	No	Yes	No

EQUIPMENT AND TECHNOLOGICAL SERVICES

14.	2	1	7
15.	5	3	52
16.	–	–	–
17.	No	No	No
18.	–	–	–
19.	No	No	No

STAFF

20.	6.5	23.05	124
21.	5.5	10.40	118
22.	4	16.77	92
23.	1.28	10.51	28
24.	17.28	60.73	362

PRINTED AND OTHER MATERIALS IN STOCK

25.	49,163	259,000	1,006,865
26.	42,216	105,000	587,406
27.	91,379	364,957	1,594,271
28	5,820	6,461	6,411

29.	11,064	18,893	108,657
30.	283	531	3,761
31.	469	28,475	81,390
32.	3	–	9
33.	67	298	2,378
34.	–	–	–
35.	–	360	30
36.	–	–	–

NUMBER OF LOANS LAST YEAR

37.	129,739	453,000	2,590,050
38.	194,320	309,000	1,705,508
39.	324,059	762,662	4,295,558
40	20,641	13,514	17,273
41.	2,358	72,008	369,880

1. GERMAN DEMOCRATIC REPUBLIC

2.	Brandenburg	Potsdam	Berlin-Pankow
3.	16,200	10,000	7,800
4.	95,000	135,000	137,800
5.	5.9	13.5	17.7

SERVICE POINTS

6.	–	1	1
7.	2	–	2
8.	4	3	10
9.	–	1	1
10.	6	5	14
11.	–	1	–
12.	18	19	3
13.	Yes	Yes	Yes

EQUIPMENT AND TECHNOLOGICAL SERVICES

14.	1	3	–
15.	1	6	–
16.	–	–	–
17.	No	No	No
18.	–	–	–
19.	No	No	No

STAFF

20.	21	115	80
21.	3	18	–
22.	1	7	3
23.	3	8	7
24.	28	148	90

PRINTED AND OTHER MATERIALS IN STOCK

25.	138,600	556,500	271,400
26.	58,900	141,200	93,900
27.	197,500	697,700	365,300
28.	2,079	5,168	2,651
29.	15,200	35,400	18,750
30.	250	1,500	222
31.	18,680	51,000	47,670
32.	–	–	–
33.	–		–
34.	–	–	–
35.	–	–	–
36.	–	–	–

NUMBER OF LOANS LAST YEAR

37.	240,300	507,200	808,650
38.	359,700	154,300	236,700
39.	600,000	661,500	1,045,350
40.	6,316	4,900	7,578
41.	–	89,500	155,150

1. GERMAN FEDERAL REPUBLIC

2.	Hannover	Duisburg	Stuttgart
3.	20,377	23,296	20,700
4.	549,414	553,276	562,232
5.	27,0	23,75	27,2

SERVICE POINTS

6.	2	1	1
7.	16	3	–
8.	2	19	13
9.	–	5	5
10.	20	28	19
11.	2	2	2
12.	–	–	3
13.	Yes	Yes	No

EQUIPMENT AND TECHNOLOGICAL SERVICES

14.	10	13	19
15.	30	85	1
16.	5	3	–
17.	No	Yes	Yes
18.	–	27	1
19.	Yes	Yes	No

STAFF

20.	82	57.5	53
21.	28	126.5	45
22.	90	7	59
23.	30	31	3
24.	230	222	160

PRINTED AND OTHER MATERIALS IN STOCK

25.	1,166,689	776,799	754,531
26.	208,903	215,840	176,449
27.	1,375,592	992,639	930,980
28.	2,503	1,794	1,656

29.	50,000	79,998	64,177
30.	2,165	1,587	1,258
31.	23,000	30,166	38,006
32.	–	–	–
33.	–	356	–
34.	14,231	–	–
35.	2,062	–	–
36.	–	–	–

NUMBER OF LOANS LAST YEAR

37.	–	698,057	–
38.	–	577,900	–
39.	2,776,147	1,275,957	2,420,844
40.	5,053	2,306	4,324
41.	–	121,715	–

1. HUNGARY

2.	Hatvan	Vas County	Budapest
3.	8,066	333,682	52,515
4.	25,087	285,498	2,060,170
5.	3.1	0.9	39.2

SERVICE POINTS

6.	–	1	1
7.	–	–	8
8.	1	6	44
9.	10	257	52
10.	11	264	105
11.	–	–	2
12.	7	20	–
13.	Yes	Yes	Yes

EQUIPMENT AND TECHNOLOGICAL SERVICES

14.	–	9	3
15.	1	8	4
16.	–	–	–
17.	No	No	No
18.	–	–	–
19.	No	No	No

STAFF

20.	6	67	418
21.	1	2	32
22.	10	70	246
23.	2	47	42
24.	19	186	738

PRINTED AND OTHER MATERIALS IN STOCK

25.	80,088	888,514	2,372,710
26.	38,955	380,791	838,013
27.	119,043	1,269,305	3,210,723
28.	4,745	4,446	1,558
29.	7,357	84,679	279,128
30.	433	5,160	1,608
31.	3,864	18,793	49,785
32.	–	125	35
33.	–	–	30,000
34.	1,652	9,087	5,750
35.	10	140	7,261
36.	–	–	–

NUMBER OF LOANS LAST YEAR

37.	43,295	731,281	3,121,214
38.	41,828	450,915	1,183,472
39.	85,123	1,182,196	4,304,686
40.	3,393	4,141	2,089
41.	102	9,000	–

1. MALAYSIA

2.	Melaka	Sabah	Kedah
3.	165,888	7,617,370	948,672
4.	400,000	1,002,608	1,439,000
5.	2.4	0.13	1.05

SERVICE POINTS

6.	–	2	–
7.	–	–	–
8.	–	16	–
9.	–	2	–
10.	1	20	4
11.	2	6	4
12.	1	–	–
13.	No	Yes	Yes

EQUIPMENT AND TECHNOLOGICAL SERVICES

14.	1	1	–
15.	–	2	–
16.	–	–	–
17.	No	No	No
18.	–	–	–
19.	No	No	No

STAFF

20.	1	21	5
21.	–	1	–
22.	10	251	30
23.	3	45	4
24.	14	318	39

PRINTED AND OTHER MATERIALS IN STOCK

25.	20,000	105,373	42,384
26.	10,000	168,381	88,385
27.	30,000	318,754	130,769
28.	75	318	91

29.	5,000	76,154	15,225
30.	150	–	28
31.	–	1,070	58
32.	–	236	–
33.	–	13	–
34.	–	–	63
35.	20	10	–
36.	–	–	–

NUMBER OF LOANS LAST YEAR

37.	38,316	1,035,591	60,306
38.	1,260	813,295	120,907
39.	39,576	1,848,886	181,213
40.	37	1,844	126
41.	–	288	–

1. UNITED KINGDOM (ENGLAND)

2.	Tameside	Cleveland	Hertfordshire
3.	10,323	58,000	163,417
4.	216,300	564,800	970,400
5.	20.9	9.7	5.9

SERVICE POINTS

6.	5	13	23
7.	4	15	9
8.	10	14	16
9.	3	–	1
10.	22	42	49
11.	1	5	12
12.	1	93	265
13.	Yes	Yes	Yes

EQUIPMENT AND TECHNOLOGICAL SERVICES

14.	6	8	27
15.	14	79	33
16.	2	–	6
17.	No	No	Yes
18.	–	–	5
19.	No	Yes	Yes

STAFF

20.	38	96	122
21.	3	2	–
22.	79.75	179	318
23.	12.43	47	27
24.	133.18	324	467

PRINTED AND OTHER MATERIALS IN STOCK

25.	436,253	501,000	–
26.	113,016	208,000	–
27.	549,269	709,000	2,320,514
28.	2,539	1,255	2,391
29.	60,187	170,448	216,390
30.	–	1,158	515
31.	26,208	34,613	55,692
32.	467	1.000	–
33.	–	–	–
34.	–	–	–
35.	2,020	6,315	1,000
36.	–	–	–

NUMBER OF LOANS LAST YEAR

37.	1,918,820	6,520,000	–
38.	296,446	1,324,000	–
39.	2,215,266	7,845,000	13,719,292
40.	10,241	13,889	14,138
41.	64,064	94,555	(in 39,40)

1. UNITED STATES OF AMERICA

2.	Thief River Falls, Minnesota	Mid-Hudson Lib. System	Suburban Lib. System Illinois
3.	1,798,200	981,684	166,500
4.	52,942	547,806	1,600,000
5.	0.03	0.55	9.6

SERVICE POINTS

6.	–	1	9
7.	–	2	27
8.	1	23	36
9.	6	43	8
10.	7	69	80
11.	1	–	1
12.	5	–	3
13.	Yes	No	No

EQUIPMENT AND TECHNOLOGICAL SERVICES

14.	2	49	100+
15.	1	31	60
16.	1	1	10
17.	No	No	Yes
18.	–	–	46
19.	No	No	Yes

STAFF

20.	2	38.2	175
21.	2	29.9	150
22.	12	60.4	540
23.	1	11.9	35
24.	17	140.4	900

PRINTED AND OTHER MATERIALS IN STOCK

25.	–	787,048	–
26.	–	307,693	–
27.	95,745	1,094,741	4,500,000
28.	1,808	2,000	2,810

29.	4,081	77,368	350,000
30.	225	3,478	5,000
31.	2,682	32,689	30,000
32.	127	3,957	10,000
33.	–	451	–
34.	5	7,380	–
35.	–	976	–
36.	–	593	–

NUMBER OF LOANS LAST YEAR

37.	133,203	834,540	–
38.	84,566	814,540	–
39.	235,351	1,649,080	9,000,000
40.	4,444	3,013	5,625
41.	–	34,997	–

1. KENYA

2.	Nairobi
3.	226,000 (approx)
4.	1 million
5.	4.0

SERVICE POINTS

6.	–
7.	–
8.	3
9.	–
10.	3
11.	–
12.	–
13.	No

1. MEXICO

2.	National Network of public libraries
3.	252 million
4.	75,567,000
5.	0.3

6.	–
7.	–
8.	5
9.	280
10.	285
11.	7
12.	–
13.	Yes

EQUIPMENT AND TECHNOLOGICAL SERVICES

14.	–	14.	–
15.	–	15.	–
16.	–	16.	–
17.	No	17.	No
18.	–	18.	–
19.	No	19.	No

STAFF

20.	3	20.	
21.	–	21.	
22.	27	22.	
23.	18	23.	
24.	48	24.	

PRINTED AND OTHER MATERIALS IN STOCK

25.	–	25.	–
26.	–	26.	–
27.	165,000	27.	1,674,683
28.	165	28.	22

29.	620	29.	–
30.	825	30.	–
31.	22	31.	10,996
32.	–	32.	–
33.	1,000	33.	–
34.	–	34.	–
35.	50	35.	–
36.	–	36.	–

NUMBER OF LOANS LAST YEAR

37.	–	37.	–
38.	–	38.	–
39.	67,072	39.	837,041
40.	–	40.	11
41.	–	41.	16,739

APPENDIX IV

STANDARDS AND GUIDELINES
RELEVANT TO SPECIFIC ASPECTS OF PUBLIC LIBRARY SERVICES

issued by specialized groups within IFLA

SECTION OF LIBRARIES FOR THE BLIND

Approved recommendations on working out national standards of library service for the blind. Washington. Library of Congress, National Library Service for the Blind and Physically Handicapped. 1983.

SECTION OF LIBRARY SERVICES TO HOSPITAL PATIENTS AND HANDICAPPED READERS

Guidelines for libraries serving hospital patients and disabled people in the community. IFLA Professional Reports no.2. 1984.

SECTION OF SCHOOL LIBRARIES

Frances Laverne Carroll and Patricia F Beilke. *Guidelines for the planning and organization of school library media centres.* Paris. Unesco. 1979.

UNESCO. *Draft school library media centre manifesto.* In *IFLA Journal* 6 (1980) 4, pp. 410–411.

ROUND TABLE ON AV MEDIA

Provision of audiovisual materials in public libraries: basic statement. 1982.

ROUND TABLE ON LIBRARY SERVICE TO ETHNIC AND LINGUISTIC MINORITIES

Guidelines for public library service to ethnic, linguistic and cultural minorities. 1985.

ROUND TABLE ON MOBILE LIBRARIES

Draft guidelines for the equipment and operation of mobile libraries. 1983.

ROUND TABLE OF NATIONAL CENTRES FOR LIBRARY SERVICES

Central services for libraries in developing countries: report of the travelling seminar, 1981. The Hague. NBLC. 1982.

INDEX

saur

A concept leads to success.
The world's publishers at a grasp

Publishers' International Directory
with ISBN Index
13th edition 1986

Managing Editor: Barbara Verrel
Editorial staff: Marianna Albertshauser/Astrid Kramuschka

1986. Volume 1: XX, 1158 pages, Volume 2: V, 1071 pages.
Bound DM 448.00
ISBN 3-598-20532-5

Handbook of International Documentation and Information,
Vol. 7

This year's PID
once again offers up-to-date, comprehensive and detailed information on publishers worldwide.
Listed are, in addition to the usual publishers, small publishing houses, publishers of periodicals, alternative publishers, institutes, organizations, private individuals, as well as microform, computer and software publishers.

PID provides information
on publishers' addresses and supplementary addresses, their distributors, and lists telephone, telex and telefax numbers, as well as telegraphic addresses. PID also covers diverse fields within the publishing industry including new areas such as video and software publications.

The success of PID
is based on a consistent principle:
Daily data maintenance, storage in a modern data bank with online access, instant updating and a brief production time made possible by computerized typesetting, guarantee the most up-to-date information.

K·G·Saur München·London·New York·Oxford·Paris

K · G · Saur Verlag KG · Postfach 71 10 09 · 8000 München 71 · Tel. (0 89) 7 91 04-0
K · G · Saur Ltd. · Shropshire House · 2-10 Capper Street · London WC 1E 6JA · Tel. 01-637-1571
K · G · Saur Inc. · 175 Fifth Avenue · New York, N.Y.10010 · Tel. (212) 982-1302
Hans Zell Publ. · An imprint of K · G · Saur Ltd. · P.O.B. 56 · Oxford OX1 3EL
K · G · Saur, Editeur SARL. · 6, rue de la Sorbonne · 75005 Paris · Téléphone 354 47 57